ALLIGATOR	BUMBLE BEE	CATERPILLAR	DINOSAUR	ELEPHANT
FLAMINGO	GIRAFFE	HIPPOPOTAMUS	IGUANA	JELLYFISH
KOALA	LION	MONKEY	NARWHAL	OWL
PEACOCK	QUETZAL	RABBIT	SLOTH	TURTLE
UNICORN	VULTURE		WHALE	XERUS
YAK		ABC	ZEBRA	

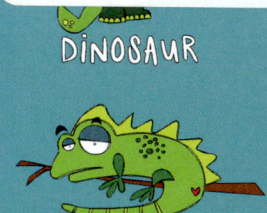

to our families: thank you for always loving and supporting our crazy ideas. to the world: be kind to one another, now more than ever. - bonjour artmoms

to my daughter grace: i've created millions of pieces of art. you, by far, are my most beautiful masterpiece. it is because of you that i know life's greatest love. i love you little one. never stop shining your big bright beautiful light. - M♥M

jer, you are my ♥heart♥ i'm so lucky to kiss you everyday! - coo

-to vivien, lex and louis: ♥je vous aime tous♥! boo-boo, loulou - both of you are amazing! i love you, ♥ you, ♥ you! - MSL

ALLIGATOR

A

AMAZING • AWESOME • AMUSING

Bumble Bee

B

BRAVE • BRILLIANT • BOLD

CATERPILLAR

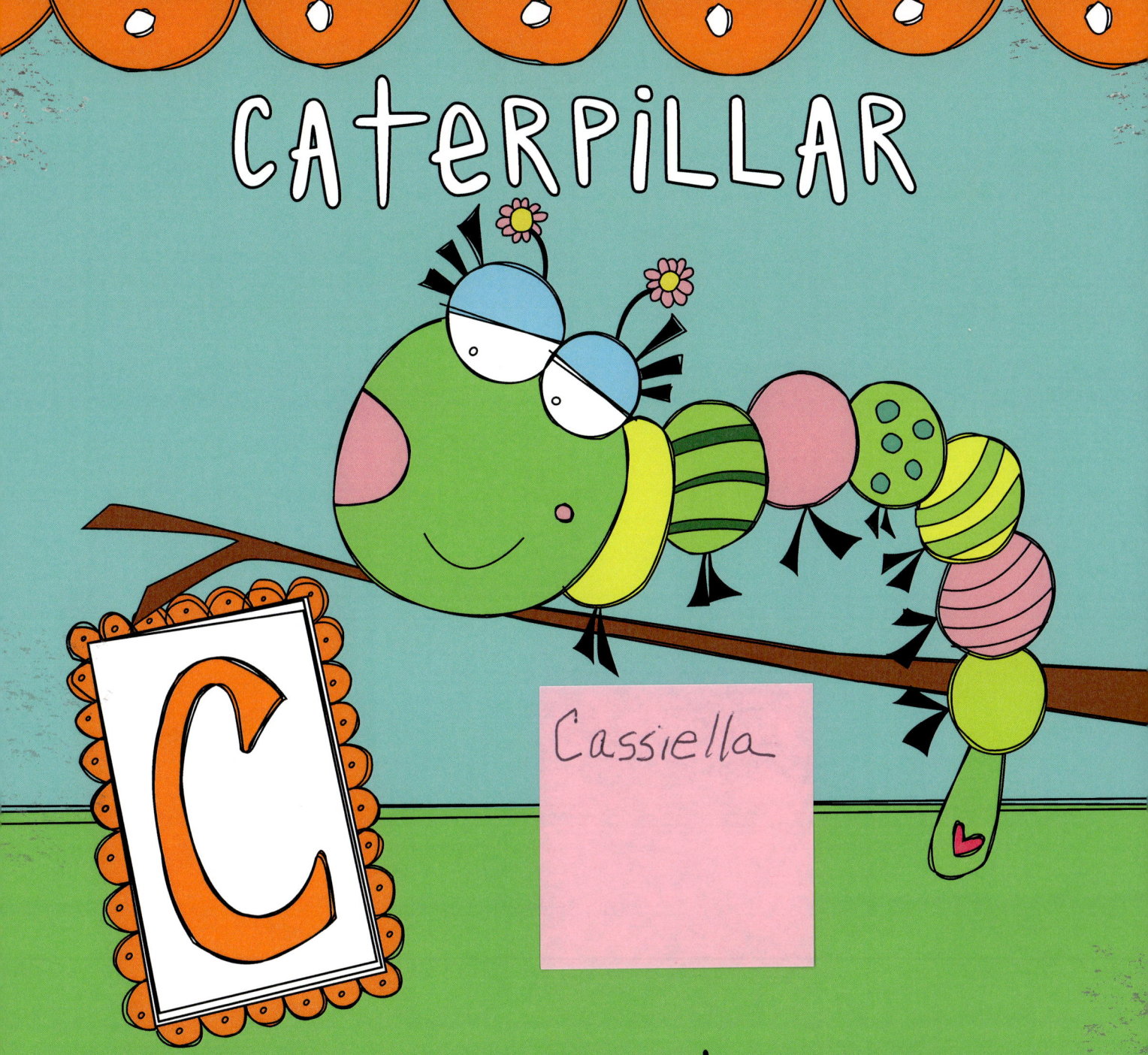

C

Cassiella

CURIOUS • CONFIDENT • COLORFUL

DINOSAUR

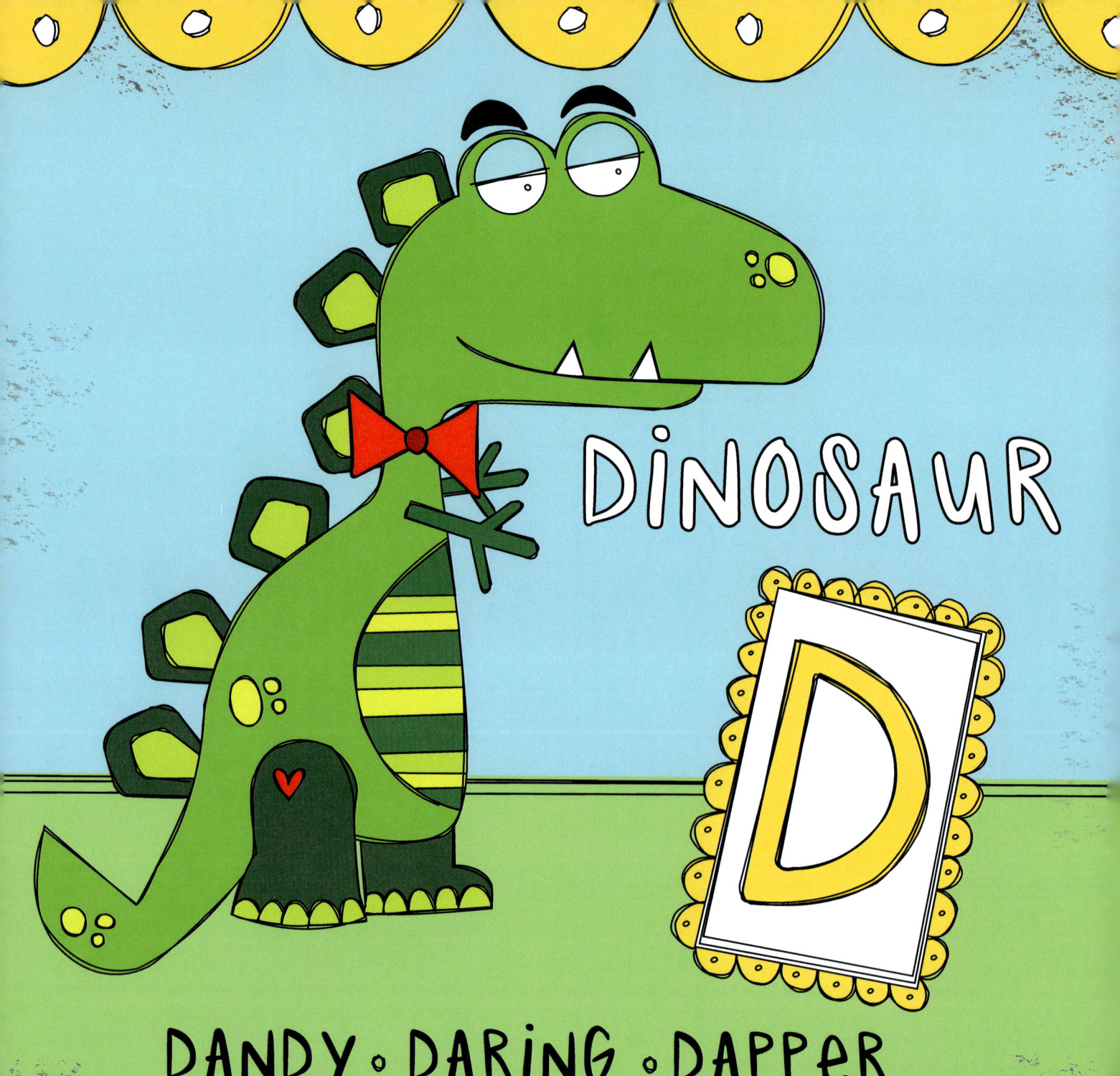

D

DANDY · DARING · DAPPER

elephant

E

elegant • encouraging • enormous

FLAMINGO

F

FANTASTIC • FUN • FLAMBOYANT

GIRAFFE

G

GENEROUS · GORGEOUS · GIGGLY

Hippopotamus

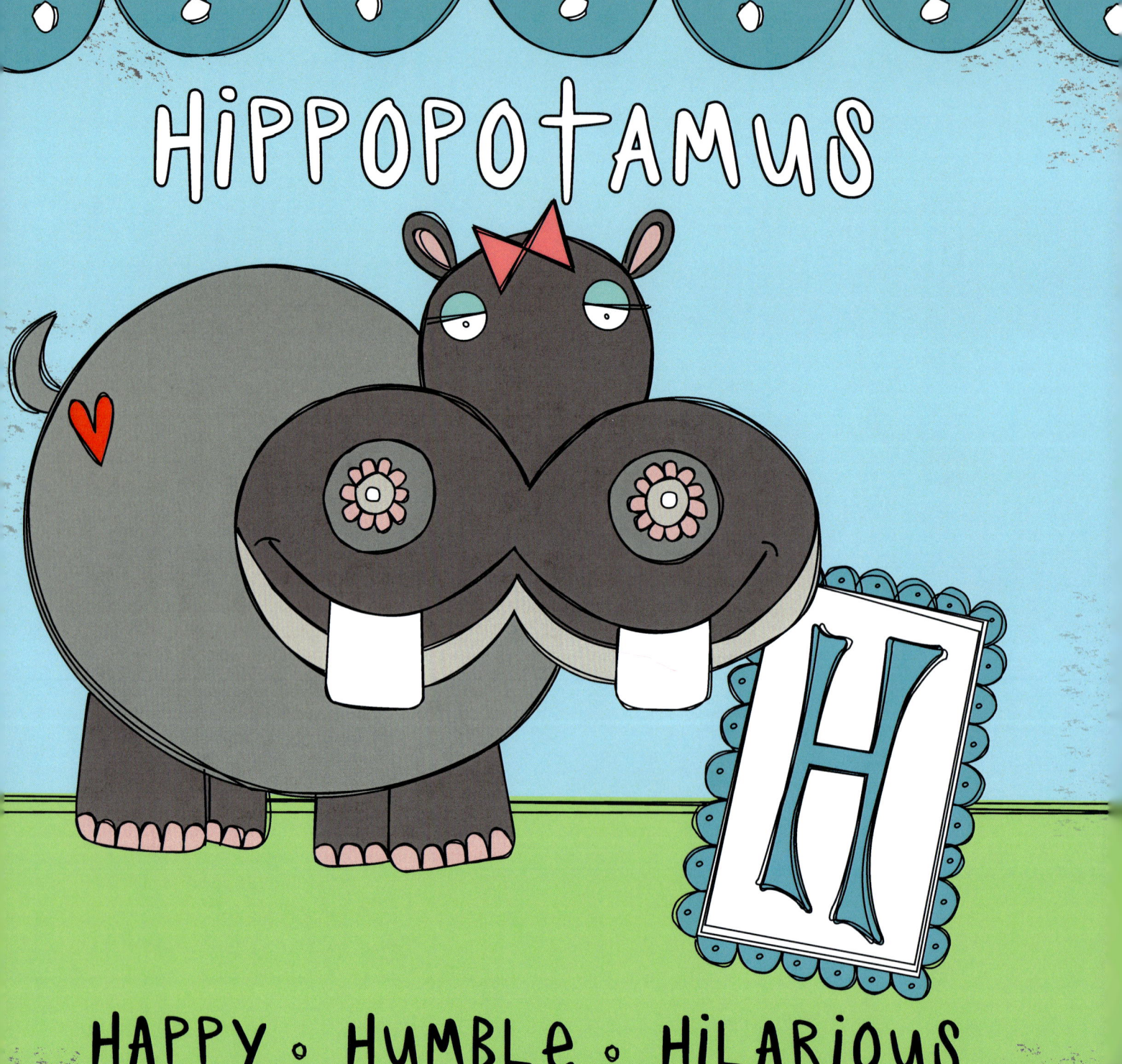

Happy • Humble • Hilarious

iguana

I

inspired . interesting . incredible

jellyfish

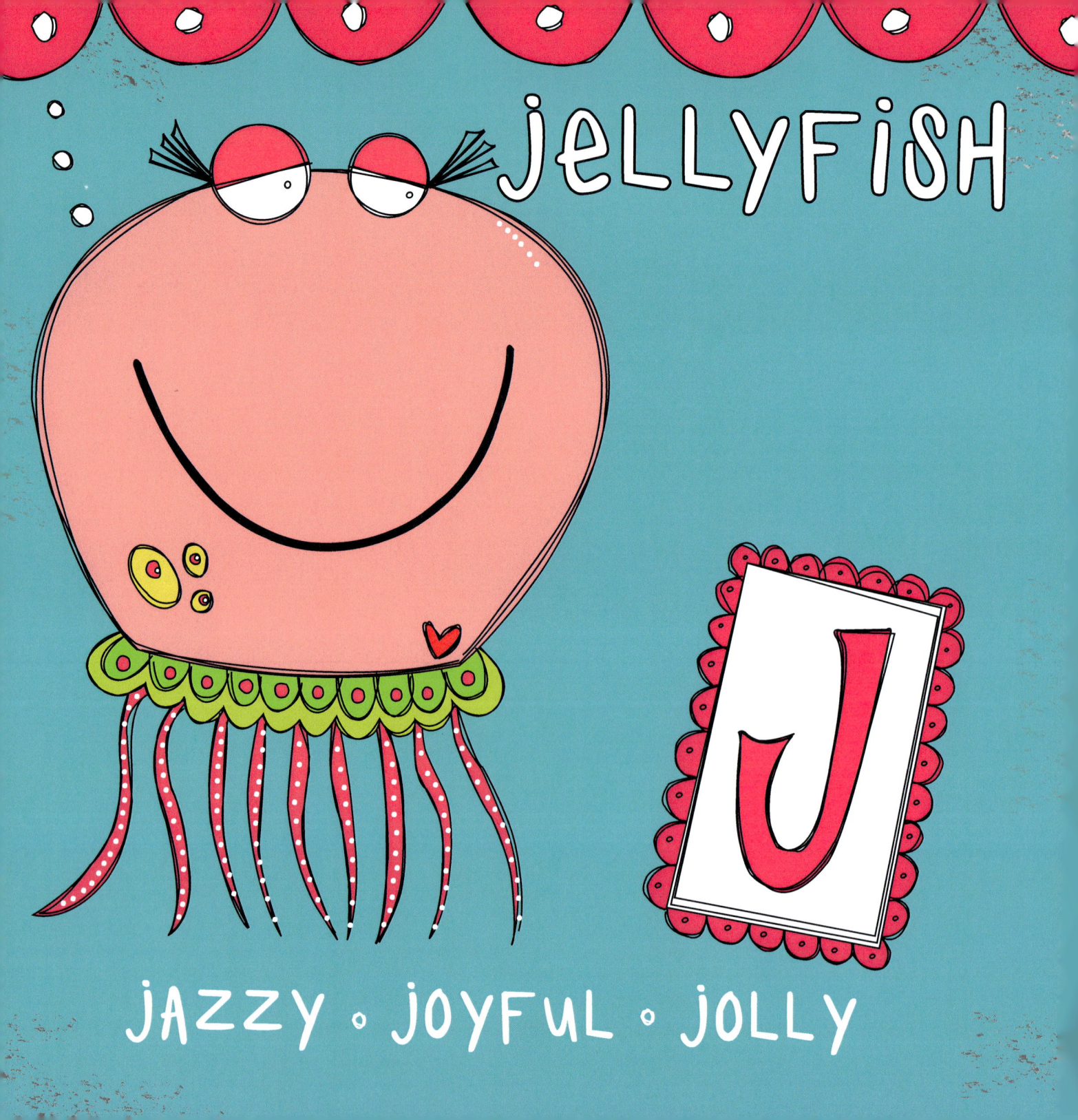

J

jazzy • joyful • jolly

KOALA

K

KIND • KNOWLEDGEABLE • KOOKY

LION

LUCKY • LEGENDARY • LOYAL

MONKEY

M

MELLOW • MISCHIEVOUS • MERRY

NARWHAL

N

NOTABLE • NICE • NOBLE

OWL

O

OPTIMISTIC • OPEN • ORGANIZED

PEACOCK

P

PATIENT • PEACEFUL • PROUD

Quetzal

Q

quiet • queenly • quaint

Rabbit

R

Remarkable • Rad • Respectful

S

SLOTH
sleepy • swell • super-duper

turtle

T

tender • thoughtful • trusty

unicorn

U

unique • unstoppable • upbeat

Vulture

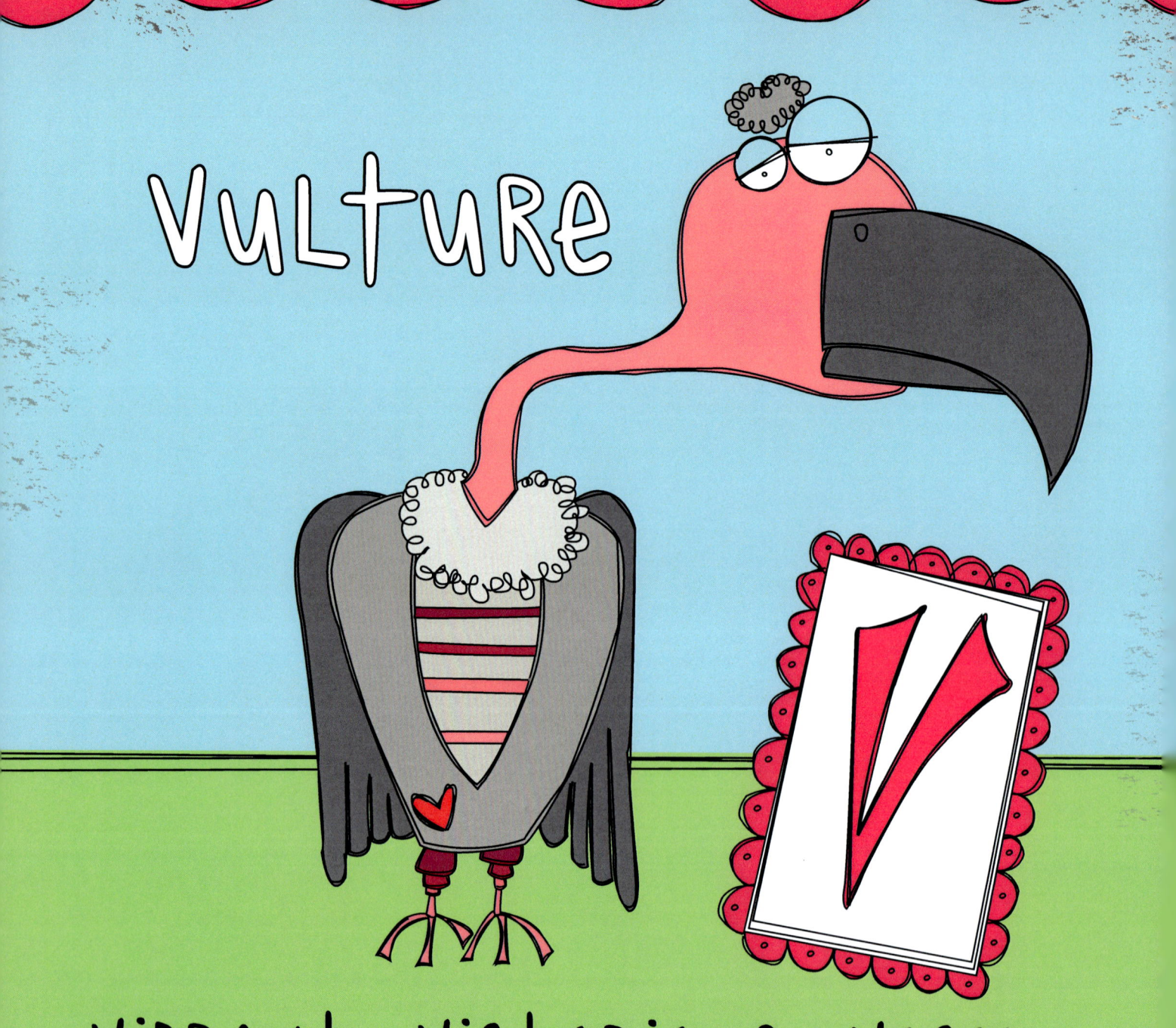

V

Vibrant • Victorious • Vocal

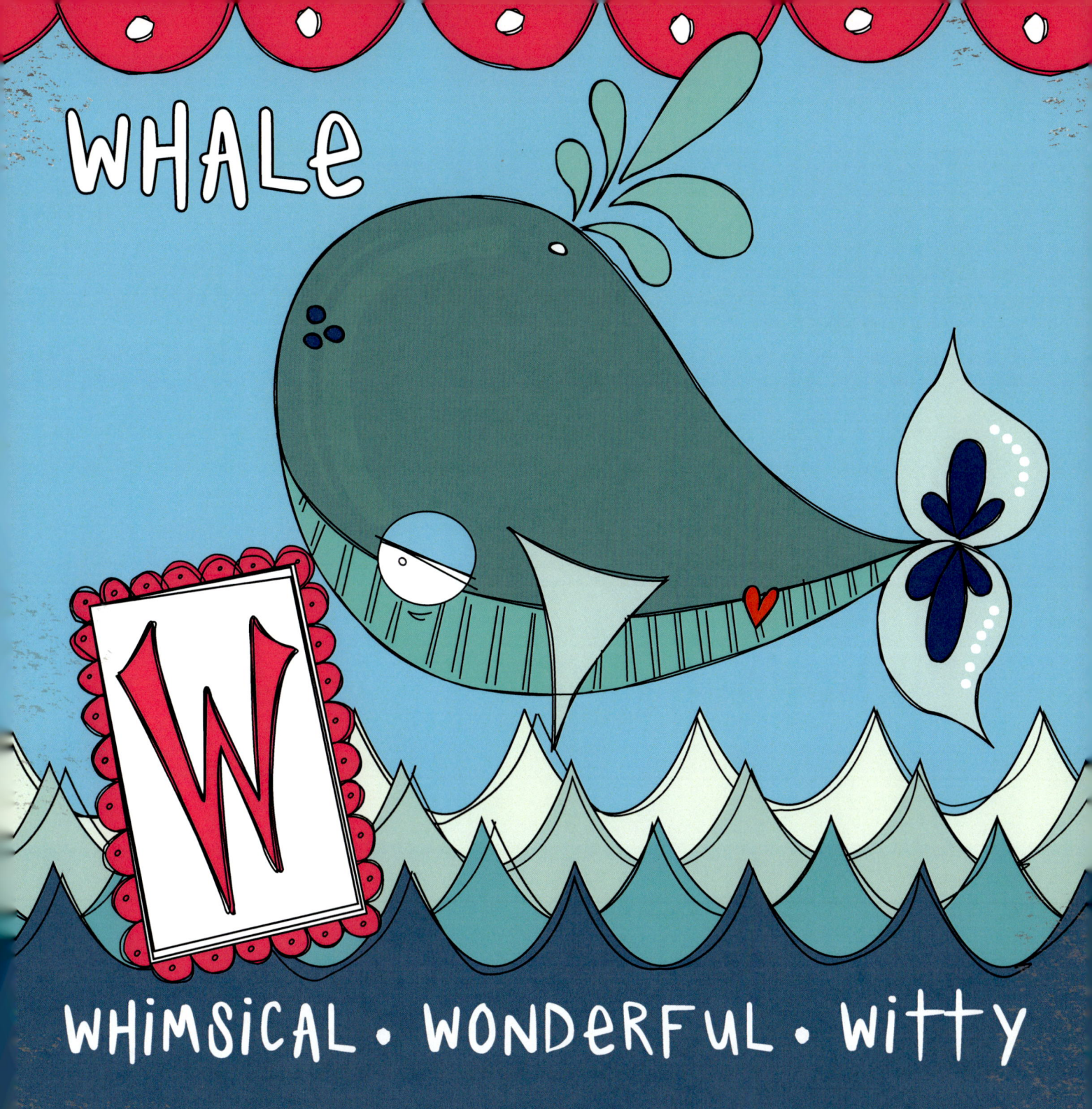

WHALE

W

WHIMSICAL • WONDERFUL • WITTY

xerus

X

excellent • extraordinary*

YAK

Y

YOUNG • YELLOWISH • YAWNY

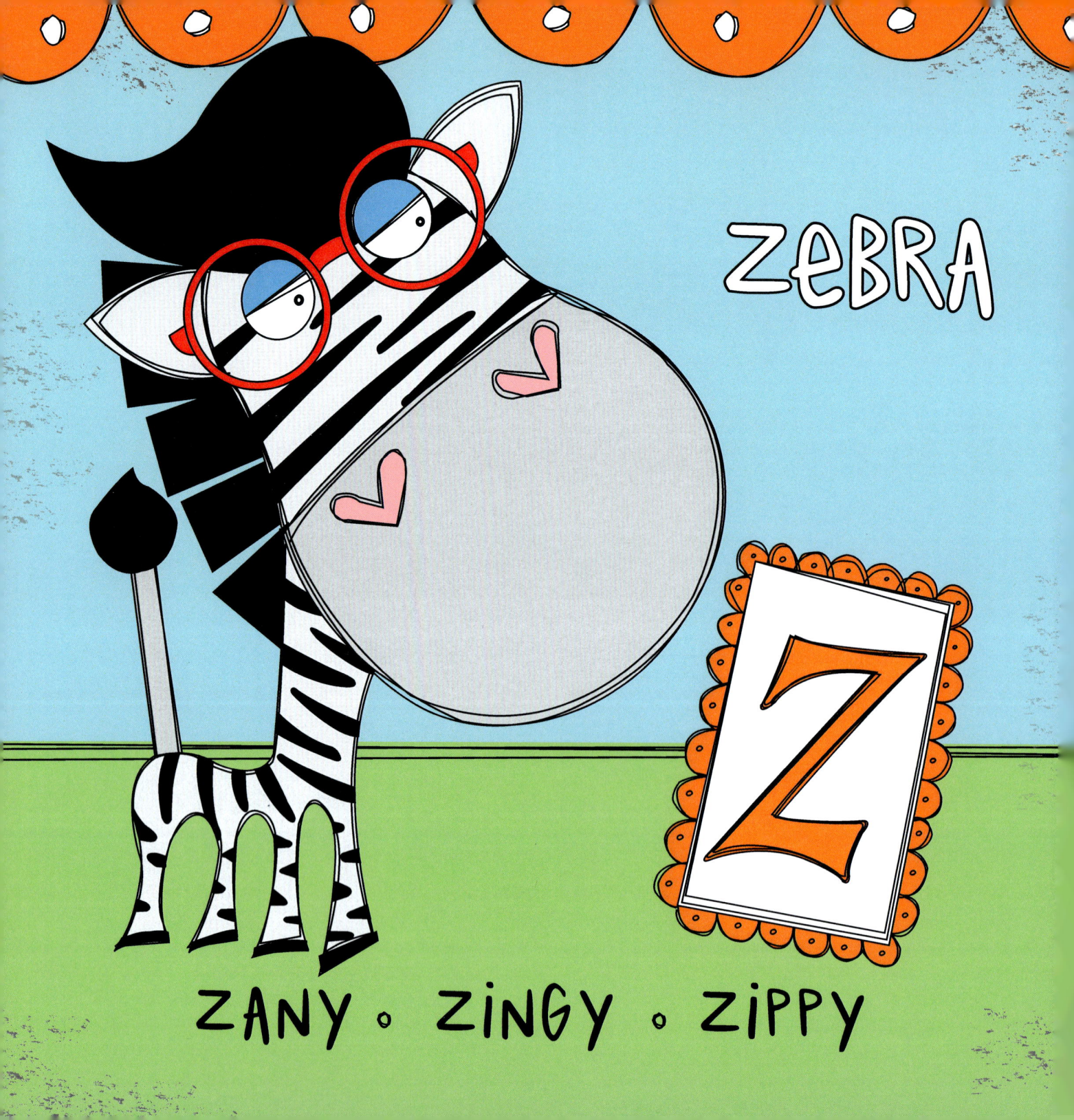

Zebra

Z

Zany • Zingy • Zippy

Question Time:

Can you find a heart on each animal?

Which animals have two hearts?

Which animals have feathers?

Which animals are in water?

Which animals are on a branch?

Which animals are wearing glasses?

Can you find the words: awesome & kind?

Which animals have horns?

Which is your favorite animal?

*Please enjoy our 'x' word substitutions. We could not find awesome enough affirmative adjectives that start with the letter 'x'. We thought these would be more fun than 'xenial' and 'xenodochial' - but feel free to add those words to your vocabulary!

DRAW YOUR FAVORITE ANIMAL HERE:

♥ IF YOU LOVED THIS BOOK - PLEASE CHECK OUT OUR COMPANION COLORING BOOK! ♥